Short
The (

LJ Stocks

COUNTRYSIDE BOOKS
NEWBURY BERKSHIRE

First published 2023
© 2023 LJ Stocks

COUNTRYSIDE BOOKS
3 Catherine Road
Newbury, Berkshire, RG14 7NA

To view our complete range of books please visit us at
www.countrysidebooks.co.uk

ISBN 978 1 84674 421 1

All materials used in the manufacture of this book carry FSC certification.

Produced by The Letterworks Ltd., Reading
Designed and Typeset by KT Designs, St Helens
Printed by Holywell Press, Oxford

Introduction

The **Chiltern Hills stretch 45 miles** across four counties. With woodland, farm fields, canals, rivers and, of course, rolling hills, it is one of the most beautiful and varied places to walk. In fact, a large portion of it has been designated an Area of Outstanding Natural Beauty. There's plenty of history hidden in the Chilterns, with Iron Age hillforts, steam railway lines, old quarries, and Britain's oldest road, the Ridgeway, which joins the ancient Icknield Way as it passes through the hills.

Our family of four started our 'Saturday Walks' as a necessary dog walk, finding local short walks that didn't require a pocketfull of bribery sweets for our two young boys! We just wanted to get out and enjoy ourselves in the beautiful countryside.

This collection of walks was put together with families in mind; those that want to explore the Chilterns without having to don full hiking gear and take provisions to last them the entire day! Perfect for younger walkers and those after a brief excursion, the shortest route is just over 1½ miles and all are under 3½ miles. There's always a spot to pause for snacks or re-energising, as well.

As you might expect, there are stunning views from the hills, alongside the expected climbs to enjoy them. However, there are routes that follow the flat valleys, circumnavigate hilltops and wind along the River Thames,

The Chilterns

with just a few gentle undulations. There's plenty to spot along the way, from fairy doors concealed in hedges and rope swings hanging from mighty oaks, as well as wildlife hidden through the woods, and of course, the ever-present red kites that the Chilterns are famous for. They'll wheel above you on most walks.

I hope you enjoy these walks as much as we do. Some of them have become our regular rambles and we love watching the seasons change around us. They may give you the opportunity to explore places you might not have seen otherwise, to experience hidden gems that give you a moment of peace and allow you to take a minute to breathe in that giant sky above us. Happy walking!

LJ Stocks

Dedication

Phil, this is as much your book as it is mine. Walking with you
is always my favourite. Thank you.
Jesse and Ezra. You are walking rock stars.
Jackson, without whom we would never have embarked on
Saturday Walks.
And Rocco. Where shall we explore next?

Publisher's Note

We hope that you obtain considerable enjoyment from this book; great care has been taken in its preparation. Although at the time of publication all routes followed public rights of way or permitted paths, diversion orders can be made and permissions withdrawn.

We cannot, of course, be held responsible for such diversion orders or any inaccuracies in the text which result from these or any other changes to the routes, nor any damage which might result from walkers trespassing on private property. We are anxious, though, that all the details covering the walks are kept up to date, and would therefore welcome information from readers which would be relevant to future editions.

The simple sketch maps that accompany the walks in this book are based on notes made by the author whilst surveying the routes on the ground. They are designed to show you how to reach the start and to point out the main features of the overall circuit, and they contain a progression of numbers that relate to the paragraphs of the text.

However, for the benefit of a proper map, we do recommend that you purchase the relevant Ordnance Survey sheet covering your walk. Ordnance Survey maps are widely available, especially through booksellers and local newsagents.

1 Christmas Common

1 ¾ miles (2.7 km)

Start: Lay-by opposite The Fox & Hounds pub. There is also parking in a large lay-by on the other side of the field on Hollandridge Lane. **Postcode:** OX49 5HL.

OS Map: 171 Chiltern Hills West. **Grid Ref:** SU714931. **what3words:** snooping.trying.welcome

Terrain: Flat woodland paths with a gentle wander downhill followed by an incline to match.

Refreshments: The Fox & Hounds is an historic country pub serving fresh local produce. Cyclists and walkers welcome. Dogs welcome in the bar. ☎ 01491 612599.

HIGHLIGHTS

Taking in some woodland walking as well as crossing open fields, there are some large pits to explore, with ditches to run through and play in. You may well spot some deer between points three and four as they graze in the enclosure.

The Chilterns

THE WALK

❶ With your back to the pub and facing the red telephone box, head left up the road to the fingerpost marked Oxfordshire and the red postbox. Follow the direction of the Stokenchurch/Chinnor marker, to join the footpath ahead of you – a grassy track between two fields. The path curves around to the right, past a wooden field gate and then continues along the edge of the field. At the fork, take the left path towards the houses, between a willow fence and a holly hedge. It emerges on to a gravel driveway by Magpie Cottage.

❷ Follow the driveway and as it curves to the left, take the footpath on your right, marked with a white arrow on a tree and 'PY3'. The path takes you into the woods, meandering through the holly bushes and yew trees. Follow the white arrows painted on the trees as they guide you through the woodland.

❸ At the T junction marked 'SH4', curve round to the right, towards pits and a long bank which marks the ancient boundary of common land. Continue to be guided by the white arrows on the trees. The pits are old quarries, and are fun to run about in and explore. Just after the ditches, follow 'SH5' heading towards the field edge. Keep the field close to your right and continue along the path. The path narrows and heads out of the woods, alongside a deer enclosure where you may spot some of the herd.

❹ You'll curve round to the right, and the path then runs along a metal fenceline, with more deer to spot. At the end of the path, you'll reach a road. Carefully cross the road and go through the metal gate on the opposite side.

❺ The arrow directs you diagonally right across the field to the next metal gate. Go through the gate, downhill towards the woodland and through another metal kissing gate into the woods. The path heads gently uphill between fences, through the woodland. The path changes to a grassy drive and leaves the woodland before crossing a country road to a gravel track.

❻ Follow the Oxfordshire Bridleway sign, which leads you up the right side of Prior's Grove Cottage. Take the woodland track immediately on your right, signed with a white arrow 'PS1 OW', into the woods, following the white arrows once more as the path winds through the woods. After

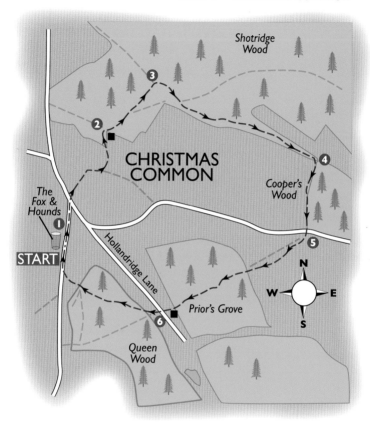

250m, the path takes you out of the woods by a willow fence and a former church (now a private residence) on your left. Turn right along the main road, walking along the verge towards The Fox and Hounds, and back to your car.

2 Warburg Nature Reserve

2½ miles (3.7 km)

Start: Warburg Nature Reserve car park - optional donation to Berks, Bucks & Oxon Wildlife Trust. **Postcode:** RG9 6BL.
OS Map: 171 Chiltern Hills West. **Grid Ref:** SU720878. **what3words:** local.yesterday.froze
Terrain: Mostly woodland tracks and well made stony paths.
Refreshments: None on the walk but there is a gated picnic area off the car park. The Rainbow Inn is a short drive to Middle Assendon, near Henley, serving pub food and real ale. ☎ 01491 574879. Henley itself is about a 15-minute drive away.

HIGHLIGHTS

Warburg Nature Reserve is tucked away between Stonor and Henley, a remote area of grassland filled with wild flowers in the summer alongside woodlands through the valleys. If you're lucky, you'll spot orchids and bluebells through warmer months, and up to 900 species of fungi through autumn. There's a visitor centre with plenty of information and activities for younger children, and additional mapped walks.

THE WALK

① From the car park head through the gate towards the information board. Follow the footpath up the hill. You'll soon reach a fork in front of a wildflower meadow and a marker for the Wildlife Walk. Take the left path. After 150m you'll meet a bench at a crossroads, follow the Wildlife Walk arrow along the path ahead. After 200m you'll reach a wooden gate. Pass through it and walk to a track.

② Turn left and follow it downhill for 80m. At the bottom of the hill, turn right on the restricted byway along a wider track, still following the Wildlife Walk arrow. Continue along the path, now ignoring the Wildlife Walk signs, as it splits away into the woods. On your left, Kitesgrove Wood stretches up the hill, and Big Ashes Plantation is on the right. Pass through wooden posts marking the bridleway and continue along the footpath. After 200m the path opens up at a convergence of five paths.

③ Turn left and head immediately through a wooden gate and into a field. Head straight on up the hill and over the field, under power lines. At the corner of the field, go through a wooden kissing gate marked the Chiltern Way and into the woods, running parallel with a field on your right. This is Stockings Plantation. The path continues to climb gently through the wood. Pass through the next wooden kissing gate, emerging into an arable field with a sign informing you this is a conservation headland. Follow the footpath as it curves to the left, hugging the edge of the woods.

④ As you reach the edge of the field, leave it and join a track that curves to the left. Follow the track downhill into the woods. After 250m, pass through

The Chilterns

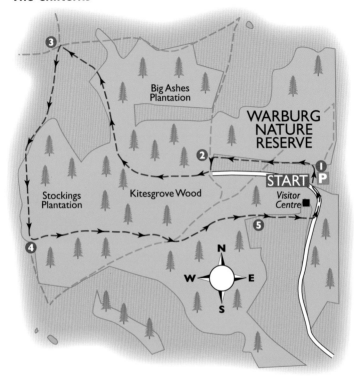

a gate and back into the nature reserve. 350m on, a track crosses your path. Carry straight on following the restricted byway purple arrow.

5 Emerge from the woods with a field on your right. Continue down the track for about 200m where you'll reach a single track road. Turn left, following the green sign with purple arrow. This is the road you drove down to get to the car park, so carefully follow it back to your car. Just before the car park you'll find Warburg Nature Reserve Visitor Centre – if it's open, pop in and find out more about the local area.

3 Fingest

2½ miles (4 km)

Start: The Chequers, Fingest. They have a small car park for patrons, or there is free parking on the road. Alternatively, park in the lay-by 150m to the east of the pub. **Postcode:** RG9 6QD.
OS Map: 171 Chiltern Hills West. **Grid Ref:** SU777911. **what3words:** lemmings.spud.connected
Terrain: Woodland paths and fields with a steep descent and some longer inclines.
Refreshments: The Chequers in Fingest serves traditional pub food and Sunday roasts. ☎ 01491 756330.

HIGHLIGHTS

The route is a lovely loop from Fingest to Cadmore End and back through woodland and open fields. There's a great viewpoint and a hill to lose your legs running down! Surrounded by medieval and Georgian cottages, St Bartholomew's church in Fingest dates from the early Norman period, and the congregation sometimes serve cake in the churchyard on a Sunday afternoon, if you're lucky!

THE WALK

❶ With your back to The Chequers, head down Chequers Lane. After 50m, you'll reach the ivy-covered Church Cottage on your right. The footpath you want is immediately after the cottage, however the public footpath sign is hidden from the road, attached to the wall of the cottage, so keep your eyes peeled! Turn right and follow the path between the brick wall and wooden fence. Continue on the path as it splits, sticking to the right, ignoring the stile. The path leads between two fields. Go through the metal kissing gate and follow the path along the right-hand edge of the field passing through the next gate which emerges onto a track.

❷ Cross the track and continue on uphill, following the power lines and into Hanger Wood. At the fork, take the left-hand path marked Public Bridleway, with a blue arrow. The path heads uphill, curving round to the left and through a holloway in the woodland. The path hugs the edge of the wood for 800m.

❸ As you meet the incoming woodland track, double back on yourself and take the public footpath deeper into the woods, following the yellow public footpath arrow.

❹ After 225m, when you reach a turning on your right, marked public footpath, with a yellow arrow, take the path into the woodland, following

the white arrows on the trees. The path heads steeply downhill to a gate as it emerges into a field with beautiful views. Go through the gate and continue steeply down the hill, staying close to the fence on your left. This is a great hill to run down, although once you start, you may not be able to stop!

5 Exit the field through three wooden gates, emerging onto a quiet lane. Turn right and head 100m towards the metal farm gates, taking the path around the metal gates and following the public footpath. After 25m, at the first marker post on your left, follow the public footpath uphill. The path splits after about 140m. Take the public footpath to the left, following the yellow arrow. On your left there are views into the valley, but keep your eyes open for wildlife in the woods to your right, you may spot squirrels, deer and hear a pheasant or two.

6 When the path reaches a T-junction at a Chiltern Way footpath sign, follow the path left, down the hill as it runs between hedges and then a brick and flint wall, to a wooden gate. The path opens onto a road. Turn left and head back to your car. If it's Sunday, you may be lucky enough to find cake being served in St Bartholomew's churchyard.

4 Frieth

3¼ miles (5 km)

Start: St John the Evangelist Church. Free parking along the road.
  Postcode: RG9 6PR.
OS Map: 171 Chiltern Hills West. **Grid Ref:** SU797902. **what3words:**
  pillow.snowboard.bookings
Terrain: Mostly flat on footpaths, some gentle hills and a couple of steps
  up to gates.
Refreshments: The Yew Tree pub is just downhill from the starting point
  (closed Tuesday and Wednesday). ☎ 01494 880077. You'll also pass
  The Prince Albert during the walk. ☎ 01494 881683.

HIGHLIGHTS

In the summer there are fields full of wild flowers all around this pretty
village. However, at any time of year this route is a lovely mixture of field
and woodland walking and you'll see gorgeous views of the surrounding
rolling hills.

THE WALK

❶ From the church, walk downhill to the corner of the churchyard. You'll
see a public footpath sign on the right side of the road directing you to a
footpath on the left, just before Flint Cottage. Take the path, pass through

a metal kissing gate and along a grassy track. In the summer, the field is transformed into a stunning wildflower meadow. At the end of the field, follow the path through two metal kissing gates to a country lane. Turn right. The road winds downhill where you'll find The Prince Albert pub, if you fancy a refreshment stop.

2 Cross the road to the public footpath marked as a permissive bridleway and follow the wide gravel track. The blue bridleway arrow guides you right, up the hill. At the end of the gravel track, continue along a narrow path through two wooden posts into the woods. At the fork in the path, take the left, heading towards the brick and flint house, visible through the trees. Lined with wild flowers in the spring and summer, the path opens up and meets a white gravel drive.

3 Turn left past Flint Lodge. After 100m you'll see a sign for Jake's Barn. Turn right and head up the hill. At the crossroads, spot the beehives to your right, but continue past Jake's Barn. The path leads downhill, between two fields and through a metal gate. Follow the path as it climbs to another gate on your right and a blue public bridleway sign.

4 Turn and continue with the hedge on your right for 120m. When you reach a gap in the hedge, before the woods, turn right and follow the path between two fields, with the hedge on your left. Walk the length of this field, to a wooden gate at the end and follow the narrow path onwards. At the end of the path, take the right-hand fork. The sheltered path brings you out between houses. Carefully cross the road and turn left, following the footpath for about 50m along the road until you reach a driveway entry.

5 Take the right track, following the gravel driveway and public footpath sign, past a row of flint and stone cottages. At the end of the drive, by Kings Corner, head into the woods, keeping the brick wall on your left. When the wall turns to the left, take the footpath to the right. Follow the undulating path through the woodland and emerge on a gravel driveway. Cross and head back into the woods, following the white arrows painted onto trees, gently descending, and crossing a wooden plank bridge. At the edge of the woodland the path opens out into a beautiful meadow. Summer walkers may spot butterflies and hear grasshoppers. Stay on the path across the meadow as it weaves through trees towards red brick houses on your left. The path joins a driveway – follow it up the hill to the road.

The Chilterns

6 Cross the road and find the public footpath to the left of the Chiltern Retreat Rural Camping driveway. Go through a pedestrian gate and follow the footpath winding through the woods. Cross the road at the end of the path and go through the metal kissing gate, taking the path to your left, uphill and across the field, towards barns in the distance. Once you meet the hedge in the middle of the field, you'll find another metal kissing gate after about 65m on your right. Go through two kissing gates and follow the narrow path between two fields. Passing the churchyard, you'll emerge onto Frieth Hill where you'll find your car.

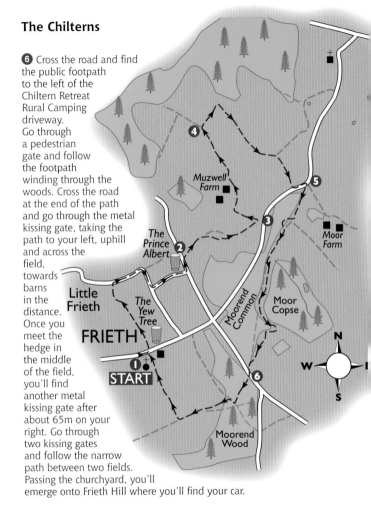

5 Medmenham

3 miles (4.5 km)

Start: Roadside parking at the far end of Ferry Lane, Medmenham.
  Postcode: SL7 2HA.
OS Map: 171 Chiltern Hills West and 172 Chiltern Hills East. **Grid Ref:**
  SU805837. **what3words:** terribly.differ.breed
Terrain: Flat field paths and grassy riverbank.
Refreshments: None on the walk. The Dog and Badger, at the top of
  Ferry Lane, on Henley Road, is over 600 years old, and serves modern,
  high quality dishes with the best British ingredients. Open daily. Dogs
  welcome in bar and garden. ☎ 01491 579944.

HIGHLIGHTS

This walk follows the Thames as it gently curves through fields. You'll start
on Ferry Lane. There was once a river crossing at the end of the road, but it
fell into disuse after the Second World War. You may pass sheep in the fields,
birds on the water and spot a range of different boats, moored up as well
as travelling along the river itself. The path along the river passes through
private land, so do stick to the footpaths, and no picnics are allowed.

The Chilterns

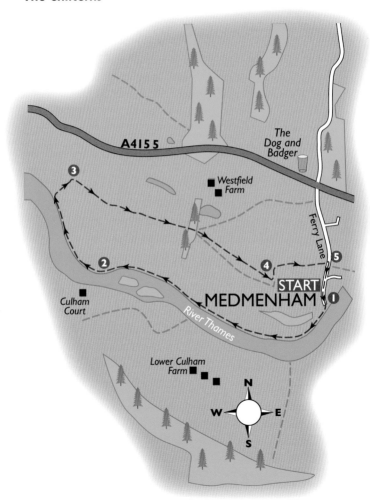

The Dog and Badger

A4155

Westfield Farm

3

2

Culham Court

4

5

START

MEDMENHAM

1

Ferry Lane

River Thames

Lower Culham Farm

N

W — E

S

18

THE WALK

1 From your car, walk down Ferry Lane to the river, take the public footpath over a bridge and curve round to the right. Pass through the gate and follow the river. This is private property, so stick to the public footpath. No picnics or BBQs are allowed, so just keep walking! You may see many different types of boats and watercraft on the river – paddle boarders, kayakers, big yachts and maybe even a paddlesteamer! At the gate that separates two fields, you can pause at the bench to watch the boats. Around the final bend of the river you'll see Culham Court in the distance on the opposite bank; a grand private residence built in 1771.

2 You'll reach a gate which leads you through a hedgeline and into an arable field. Follow the left edge of the field, with the river hidden behind the hedge, as it curves up to pass by houses.

3 A gap in the hedge and a footpath sign meet you at the end of the houses on your left, at a bend in the road beyond. Turn right and walk under powerlines, straight across the field. Cross the track by utility buildings, and continue straight across the second field. Pass over a track and cross the third field, before crossing through a thick wooded hedgeline and following the right-hand footpath across a fourth field.

4 After 600m you'll reach the edge of the field, follow the path as it curves right and then turns sharp left. The path leads to a gate which takes you winding through the woodland, alongside a fence. You'll reach a tarmac drive – cross it and head through the gate and into the field opposite. Stick close to the right edge and at the end of the field, pass through a hedgeline, into an area of scrubland. Continue straight as the path brings you out on Ferry Lane.

5 Turn right and head back down the road to find your car.

6 Hurley

1¾ miles (2.6 km)

> **Start:** Hurley village car park. If full, free parking along the High Street, with seasonal restrictions. Park on the High Street and head down to the starting point at the village car park. The walk brings you directly back to the High Street. **Postcode:** SL6 5NB.
>
> **OS Map:** 172 Chiltern Hills East. **Grid Ref:** SU825840. **what3words:** magic.coconuts.scanty
>
> **Terrain:** Well made footpaths and gravel towpaths.
>
> **Refreshments:** Hurley Lock Tea Shop next to the lock, open spring to autumn Wednesday to Sunday for drinks, snacks, cakes and ice creams. The Olde Bell on the High Street is a short detour from the walk, and serves seasonal local produce from their kitchen garden. Parts of the inn date back to 1135. ☎ 01628 969790.

HIGHLIGHTS

A pretty walk by the River Thames, taking in Hurley Lock and surrounding fields. There's space to picnic on the island by the lock and watch the boats pass through, and there's also a tea shop, open spring to autumn. Excellent boat-spotting and duck-feeding opportunities, so remember your duck food!

THE WALK

❶ Head out of the car park towards the church and turn left following the path past Tithecote Manor down a narrow paved footpath between houses, following a public footpath sign. When you reach the end of the path, head up the steps and over the bridge. There's also an accessible option for pushchairs which gets you up onto the bridge. Cross the bridge and you'll reach Hurley Lock.

❷ Continue along the footpath, with lots of ducks to see and boats to watch. Pause here; there's plenty of benches and grassy spaces for a picnic, and watch the boats coming in and out of the lock. You can also sample some delicious refreshments from the Hurley Lock Tea Shop. When the lock-keeper is on duty, it's great fun to watch them open and close the lock gates and see the boats rise and fall. Continue past the lock-keeper's hut, through the gates and onto a gravel path.

❸ Follow the path up and across the bridge, down the other side and along the Thames Path as it curves to the left. Before you get to the next bridge, you'll pass through a wooden gate with woodland on your right.

❹ At the acorn sign, take the path on your right, keeping the wooden fence on your left, until you reach a metal kissing gate leading you out onto a gravel track and into fields.

❺ Turn right, walking through the fields, ignoring any footpaths signed off the track.

❻ The gravel track turns into a tarmac road. As it bears round to the right, leave it on a signed footpath to your left, between two fields and under horse chestnut trees. In the autumn, this is a great spot for conker collecting and blackberry picking.

The Chilterns

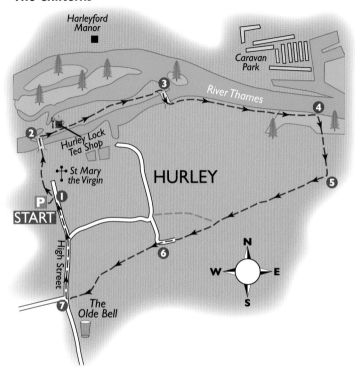

7 The path continues between two wooden fences and emerges on Hurley High Street, by The Olde Bell. Stop here if you fancy a refreshment break at the pub, otherwise carefully cross the road to the footpath on the opposite side and turn right, heading back along the High Street. If you parked on the High Street, it's time to find your car. If not, head down the road to the village car park. You'll pass a blue plaque on your left at Hurley Manor; the site of OSS Station Victor, a clandestine radio station communicating between London and secret agents in occupied Europe in the 1940s. Pass Hurley Village Shop – stop here if you fancy an ice cream – at the end of the road, you'll find the car park on your left.

7 Bledlow

3¼ miles (5.3 km)

Start: Car park behind the Lions of Bledlow pub. Additional parking on
Church End. **Postcode:** HP27 9PE.
OS Map: 181 Chiltern Hills North. **Grid Ref:** SP776019. **what3words:**
reading.sinkhole.worth
Terrain: Field paths, some muddy. Well made woodland tracks with a
steep ascent at the halfway mark and a steep descent at the end. A
few stiles.
Refreshments: The Lions of Bledlow is a 16th-century Free House
with a large open fire serving pub food and real ales. Dogs welcome.
☎ 01844 343345.

HIGHLIGHTS

Taking in some glorious Chiltern views, this walk leads you from Bledlow to
Chinnor and back, and for a part, follows the Chinnor to Princes Risborough
railway line. Here you may spot steam trains, or the shuttle train – make
sure you give it a wave!

THE WALK

❶ From the car park, turn right, down the lane to a wooden gate on your
left opposite the pub. This leads to a path that runs diagonally across a
farmer's field to a gate in the opposite corner. Pass through the gate and

The Chilterns

continue straight ahead on the track marked with blue public bridleway arrows and 'Swan's Way' bridleway signs. After 350m you'll reach metal farm gates on the right and left of the path. On your right there's also a public footpath sign and a wooden stile.

❷ Cross the stile into the field, following the path next to the fence, the length of the field. Cross the stile out of the field, next to a telegraph pole. Then cross a second stile onto a narrow path between fields to another stile. The path then opens up to a grassy track and to another stile, through Wainhill Farm and another stile, to a road.

❸ Turn right here and head down the road. A short detour further down the track will take you to a railway crossing and the Icknield Line Steam Railway – see if you can spot the steam train that runs between Chinnor and Princes Risborough at the weekends. Otherwise, from the farm, walk across the road diagonally to the right, to a public footpath next to Thatched Cottage on your left. Head down the track and follow the path as it turns left. It winds through the trees, emerging in an arable field that runs parallel with the railway line across the field on your right. After nearly 700m, the path narrows between hedges and meets a flint path.

❹ Turn left here and head uphill between hedges for 400m where the path meets the Ridgeway.

❺ Turn left, following the Ridgeway past houses and under trees, with a nature reserve on your right. This is the historic Icknield Way, an ancient trackway that runs from Norfolk to Wiltshire. The path opens up into open woodland. Continue for ½ mile, ignoring any paths to your left or right.

6 As you reach brick cottages, there is a convergence of paths. Carry on with the cottages to your right, the path passes to the left of them. Head back into the woods as the path curves round with beautiful views over the valleys to your left.

7 After ½ mile, at the wooden fingerpost, turn left, leaving the Ridgeway and heading down the hill between two metal posts, following the bridleway sign. Pause here and admire the views across the valleys to the Chiltern Hills on the opposite side. In just under ½ mile, the path emerges onto a track. Carry on straight, following the green Bridleway Bledlow sign. After another 100m, head down the track, where you'll find your car in the car park on the right.

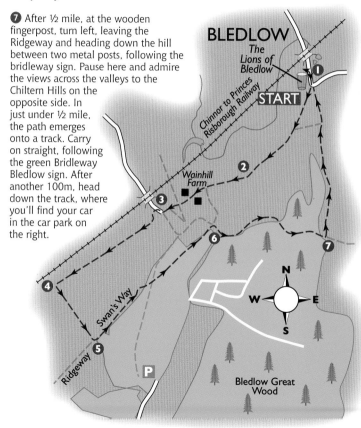

BLEDLOW

The Lions of Bledlow

Chinnor to Princes Risborough Railway

START

Wainhill Farm

Swan's Way

Ridgeway

P

Bledlow Great Wood

8 Lacey Green
3 miles (4.8 km)

Start: Lay-by on Pink Road outside The Whip Inn. **Postcode:** HP27 0PG.
OS Map: 181 Chiltern Hills North. **Grid Ref:** SP818007. **what3words:**
absorb.blush.power
Terrain: Flat field paths with some fairly overgrown. One muddy descent.
A few stiles.
Refreshments: The Whip Inn is a traditional country pub serving hearty
meals. Dogs and walkers welcome. ☎ 01844 344060.

HIGHLIGHTS
There are plenty of curiosities to spot on this walk – fairy doors, sculptures,
a sailing ship and an elf lookout hiding in the hedgerows. It also takes you
through Widmer Farm Park. You can find it down Pink Road if you fancy a
proper visit to feed the animals. There's also a windmill behind The Whip
that you can see on the very first part of your walk. Dating from around
1650, it is the oldest smock windmill in the country and is open April to
September for a small donation.

THE WALK

1 Head to Main Road and turn left. Down the lane behind the pub you'll see Lacey Green Windmill. Take a little detour here if you wish to see it close up. Walk along Main Road towards the bus shelter and just before you reach it, turn through the metal gate on your left, signed The Chiltern Way. Follow the path straight across the field. You'll see the windmill over the hedge to your left. Head through the next gate across the next field and then another metal gate and straight across this field, following the public footpath. At the tree just past the gate you may well spot a fairy door.

2 This field heads down towards a livery and Widmer Farm Park where you'll spot many different animals. Pass through a kissing gate into a paddock and follow the path diagonally across it to the white stile. Cross the stile and turn left up the gravel track between the paddocks. At the end of the track, as you reach the next field, cross the stile, go under the powerlines and across the grassy field, following the footpath to an arched gap in the hedge with a metal gate. Go through the gate and diagonally right across the field towards a wooded hedgerow. You'll soon see a metal gate and a sign marking The Chiltern Way. Pass through the gate and turn left onto Grim's Ditch, Iron Age earthworks that lead you downhill to a tarmac road.

3 Turn right here and follow the restricted byway. At Lily Farm, the tarmac road becomes an unmade track and then a woodland path. After 400m, as the path starts to climb, you'll find a wooden gate on your right.

4 Go through the gate, following the public footpath around the edge of the field. The path winds downhill through the woods, hugging the edge of the field. It can be a little overgrown with stinging nettles in the summer. After about 200m you'll meet a gate and the path turns uphill, still running parallel with the fence on your left. About 250m on, the path meets a track. Turn right and follow the track downhill towards stables.

5 At the end of the track, turn right, following the restricted byway, towards the brick and flint house. You'll see an impressive ship in the garden, followed by some fun sculptures in the hedgerow. The track turns into a tarmac road, and as it begins to climb, you'll see a public footpath into the woods on your left, marked public right of way.

6 Turn off the track here and head through the woods, uphill and back

The Chilterns

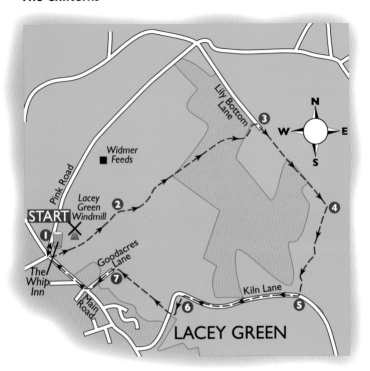

along Grim's Ditch. At the top of the hill by the houses, follow the path as it curves round to the right and hits a gravel track. Cross the track and head to the public footpath between hedges. You'll find an elf lookout on your left along this track – eyes up!

7 At the end of the path, go through a metal gate and turn left, following the track up to the road. Goodacres Lane will lead you back up to Main Road. Turn right and head back along the road to The Whip and your car.

9 Bradenham

2½ miles (3.8 km)

Start: Car park on a lane off Rectory Lane, past the cricket club, next to Bradenham St Botolph Church. **Postcode:** HP14 4HF.

OS Map: 172 Chiltern Hills East. **Grid Ref:** SU827969. **what3words:** brand.sadly.cooks

Terrain: Well worn footpaths through the woods, some hills and a few gates.

Refreshments: None on the walk. The Red Lion Tea Room sits at the bottom of Bradenham Wood Lane, a short detour from the end of the walk and serves sandwiches, ploughman's lunches and cream teas. ☎ 01494 565554.

HIGHLIGHTS

A lovely stroll through the woods, hills and meadows around Bradenham in National Trust land. Bluebell woods to enjoy in the spring, and wildflower meadows in the summer months. The views over the Chilterns are simply wonderful, and you may spot a train passing in the valley.

THE WALK

❶ In the back right-hand corner of the car park, you'll find your footpath, marked with a National Trust sign, saying 'No Unauthorised Vehicles Beyond

The Chilterns

This Point'. Follow the wide gravel track uphill before it bears left and forks. Take the left path, following the brick wall. The track splits again at the top of the hill. Keep to the left fork, not up the hill, and continue on this path, ignoring any paths off to the left or right. The path continues to climb gently through the mixed woodland for 400m. Merging with a path from the right, continue gently down towards the road.

❷ At the bottom of the hill, turn left and head down to the road. This is a busy main road, so cross carefully and head back into the woods on the other side, passing the National Trust 'Bradenham' sign. Ignore any paths off the main track and follow the National Trust horseshoe arrow signs. The path heads downhill to a dip and uphill again. These woods are full of bluebells in the spring.

❸ At the top of the dip, 20m later, take the left-hand path as it winds downhill again to a wooden gate. Go through the five-bar gate and turn right, heading downhill along the edge of the tree-lined field. You may like to pause here on the log bench and admire the beautiful views over the Bradenham estate. See if you can spot the polo horses grazing in their paddocks and a train passing in the valley beyond. Head down the hill carefully following the grassy track. Go through the hedgeline and continue straight until you meet the gravel track.

❹ Cross the track and head uphill to a gate in the hedgeline and up four wooden steps, ignoring the gate to the right. Keep on straight to the top of the hill. In the distance, to your left, you may see the famous golden ball on top of St Lawrence's Church at West Wycombe. Follow the path, keeping close to the treeline on your right as it curves around the top of the hill, with benches on your right and beautiful panoramic views over to West Wycombe. Descend to a metal farm gate and kissing gate. Head through the gate and down the small hill to the track.

❺ Turn hard left down the track, following the fence line along a public footpath. At the bottom of the field, you'll meet a farm lane. Cross the lane and head straight along a mown grass path, running parallel with the farmer's field, following a yellow public footpath sign. Keep following the grass track, with the fence on your right until you reach a five-bar gate, pass through that and a smaller field before reaching another gate which emerges on to a gravel drive, with the road beyond.

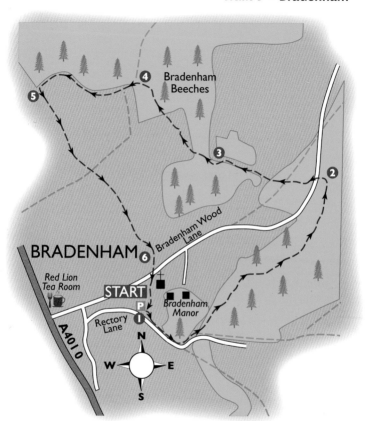

6 Follow the driveway to the road, carefully cross it and head up the path with Bradenham Manor and the church on your left and the cricket field on your right, back to the car park and your car. There are benches dotted around the cricket pitch, great for a picnic, or head down Bradenham Wood Lane to The Red Lion for refreshments.

10 **Downley**
2 miles (3.4 km)

Start: Plomer Green Lane, by the cricket club. Park in the lay-by or roadside. **Postcode:** HP13 5YQ.
OS Map: 172 Chiltern Hills East. **Grid Ref:** SU847956. **what3words:** elaborate.drag.nail
Terrain: Field and woodland footpaths. Very muddy for much of the year. One steep incline up a tarmac drive.
Refreshments: Le De Spencers Arms is a cosy little pub with home-cooked food, child-friendly garden and play area. ☎ 01494 535317.

HIGHLIGHTS
This walk is a loop from Downley Common through Naphill Common and past some interesting dips, locally known as 'The Dells'. The old clay pits probably once served the brick kiln on the Common, but today they make excellent bike ramps for mountain bikers and BMXers.

THE WALK
❶ Take the path marked public footpath to the right of the Downley Sports Pavilion. The path starts as a driveway to Blacksmiths Cottage. Follow the

path through the metal kissing gate to your left and straight across the field to the next metal kissing gate in the hedge. Go through the gate, emerging in an arable field and continue straight with the hedgeline on your right, along the length of the field. Views to your left stretch over to West Wycombe and the golden ball which sits on top of St Lawrence's church on the Dashwood estate. The hollow ball has seating for six people and was used by members of the infamous Hell Fire Club, founded by the eccentric Francis Dashwood.

2 Follow the path downhill, under overhead powerlines and into a small woodland where you'll see plenty of bluebells in May. Keep on the path as it takes you steeply down to a grassy hollow. Turn left down the grassy track until you reach a tarmac drive.

3 Turn right and follow the drive all the way up to the farm

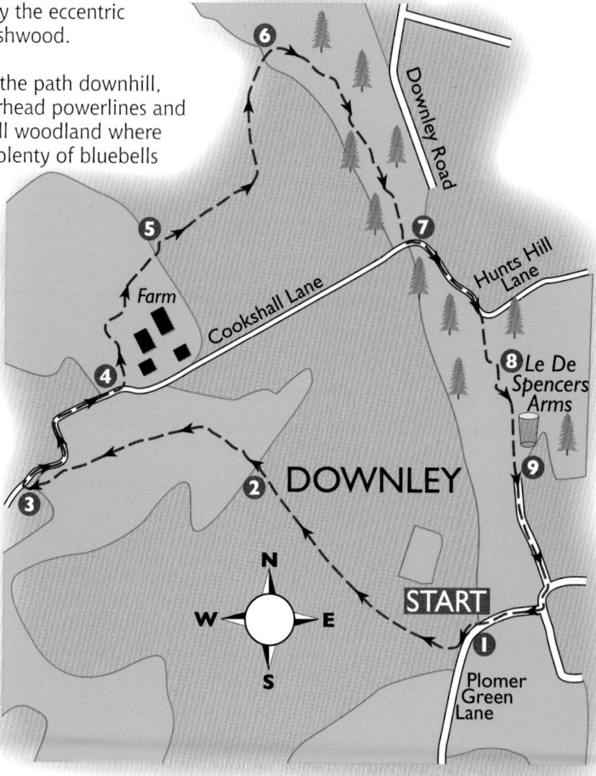

Downley Road

Hunts Hill Lane

6

5

Farm

Cookshall Lane

7

8 Le De Spencers Arms

9

4

3

2

DOWNLEY

N

W — E

S

START

1

Plomer Green Lane

The Chilterns

at the top, where you'll meet a public footpath sign, before the buildings. Turn around for a moment to take in more beautiful views over to West Wycombe.

❹ Turn left, passing in front of the farm buildings as the path curves round to the right. Follow it all the way round as it passes through farm gates and then through a field, emerging at another farm pathway. You may well see a lot of pheasants and partridges, as the farm breeds them and releases them for local shoot days.

❺ Cross the path and head straight on, keeping the hedgerow to your right. It's the only path you can take as the other paths are marked 'Private, No Public Right of Way'. Walk two sides of the field, turning left at the corner, and follow the path through the hedge, through a metal gate and into the woods.

❻ Head to the path and turn right, following it through the woodland. You'll come across a large oak tree where multiple paths converge, and if you're lucky, there may be a tyre swing to pause at and enjoy. Continue on the path back into the woodland. The path passes a pond to your left which is fun to explore, before emerging on a gravel track.

❼ Turn left and follow it as it winds under trees and past houses until you reach a small parking area at the edge of the wood. Through the car park and into the woods, follow the main footpath until you reach some dips.

❽ This is Downley Dells, an old clay pit, which now provides natural ramps for bikers to enjoy. There is a path that skirts the dips to the left, so follow that in a straight line through the woods and emerge onto a gravel path which turns into a driveway for residents. On your left is Le De Spencers Arms – stop here for some well-earned refreshments. Dogs are welcome, on a lead, and it has a lovely garden.

❾ The gravel driveway curves to the right and turns into a tarmac road. Follow this to the common where you'll find your car. There's plenty of space for children to play on the common, or you can just sit and watch the red kites and enjoy a picnic.

11 Weston Turville

3 miles (4.6 km)

Start: Church Lane, near number 28 (Sunny Cottage), off Bates Lane. Roadside parking. **Postcode:** HP22 5SU.
OS Map: 181 Chiltern Hills North. **Grid Ref:** SP859106. **what3words:** quail.tropic.position
Terrain: Flat field paths and a well made canal towpath. Farm fields may have livestock.
Refreshments: The Chequers Inn has a traditional bar and a fine dining restaurant. (No children under 6 after 4pm) ☎ 01296 613298.

HIGHLIGHTS

This walk takes in part of the Wendover Arm of the Grand Union Canal that skirts RAF Halton. You'll also cross farmland and the Weston Turville Nature Reserve and you may spot Weston Turville Reservoir in the distance.

THE WALK

❶ Start your walk at the road sign 'Brookside' behind Sunny Cottage. Head up the path to the right of the Brookside sign, following the public footpath. The path soon crosses a narrow bridge over a stream and through a wooden kissing gate into a field. The public footpath then heads diagonally left across the field, to a wooden stile in the opposite corner. Cross the stile

The Chilterns

and walk diagonally across the next arable field, following the well-worn footpath. Far in the distance, in front of you looms Wendover Woods, a lovely Forestry Commission managed woodland.

❷ Cross the next stile and head diagonally right across the field towards the red-roofed barns. Exit the field through the metal gate and cross the small wooden bridge, pass through the metal gate and into the next field. Head to the far left-hand corner of the field where you'll cross another little wooden bridge and head over a wooden stile into the next field. Walk along the left side of this field to another metal gate which leads you out onto a driveway.

❸ Carefully cross the main road to the wide grass verge on the other side, and turn right past the entrance to Halton Airfield and onto a paved footpath. Pass Halton Village Hall and the old school on your right with intricately bricked chimney stacks.

❹ After 300m, just before you reach the bridge, cross the road and head down the footpath marked 'The Wendover Arm Grand Union Canal'. As you continue along the towpath, keep an eye and ear out for troops training as RAF Halton is on the other side of the canal. You might see the buildings through the hedges. Keep along the towpath for just over ½ mile.

❺ Just before you reach a bridge marked with number 10, turn right, following the yellow permissive footpath arrow, away from the canal. This takes you through private woodland, so stick to the marked footpath, before emerging onto Halton Lane.

❻ Turn right through a lay-by, and from that lay-by turn right again, through a wooden gate, doubling back into Weston Turville Reservoir Nature Reserve. Follow the path through the woods and then out as it opens up onto a big arable field, following the yellow public footpath arrow. As

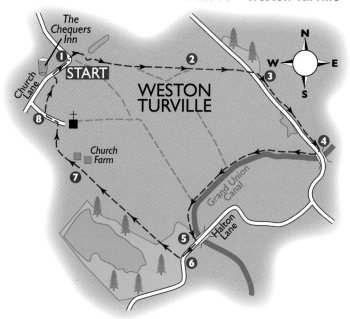

you walk across this field, to the left is Weston Turville Reservoir where you may spot some boats.

7 At the end of the field, next to the green farm buildings, cross the stile and, sticking to the wooden fence on your right, walk the length of the field. Through an old metal gate you'll reach the driveway to Church Farm. Turn left to the end of the drive, where you'll see the church on your right. Turn left, past the pretty Manor Cottage.

8 After 80m, just before a big horse chestnut tree and the bridge, turn right down a public footpath running next to the stream for about 300m. The path leads you over a concrete bridge and up a path next to a fenceline, to the road beyond. Emerge on Church Lane where you'll see The Chequers Inn for a refreshment stop, or turn right and find your car.

12 Kings Ash

3¼ miles (4 km)

Start: Lay-by or verge on Chesham Lane, Kings Ash. Park outside 'Southside' house, next to a public footpath marked Chiltern Link. **Postcode:** HP16 9NP.

OS Map: 181 Chiltern Hills North. **Grid Ref:** SP889056. **what3words:** unframed.securing.haunts

Terrain: Woodland paths, some fairly long, steep inclines.

Refreshments: None on the walk. The Firecrest in Wendover is a three-minute drive away and is a lovely country pub serving a hearty seasonal menu. Dog friendly. ☎ 01296 628041.

HIGHLIGHTS

Taking in some of the Ridgeway, this walk has a lovely mix of woodland and open field walking. You'll also spot an Ordnance Survey Triangulation Pillar and take in beautiful views across the Chilterns. You'll have to climb for them though!

THE WALK

❶ From the lay-by, take the public footpath next to Southside, marked Chiltern Link, through a wooden gate, to a metal kissing gate and on into a grassy field. Stick to the left edge of the field and head towards the woods. Pass through another metal gate and walk the curved edge of the field, keeping the woodland close on your right. Follow the path to a telegraph pole and a wooden gate.

❷ Go through the kissing gate, emerging on the driveway of a big grey house. Follow the footpath sign marked Wendover down the grassy pathway in front of the house to a wooden gate. Pass through and head downhill, continuing on the Chiltern Link footpath. The path leads you through the woods.

❸ At the bottom of the hill you'll see a fingerpost. Turn right, following the Ridgeway Bridleway sign, back into the woods. The path appears to fork, take the left-hand path, following the blue arrow and acorn sign, past the Ridgeway National Trail map. At the next fork, continue to follow the blue bridleway arrow and acorn which takes you uphill for about 500m. As the path reaches the top of the hill, you'll meet another finger post. Take the branch off to the right up the hill, following the yellow footpath sign and the white arrows marked on trees. The short path takes you to a woodland track.

❹ Turn left onto the wider track and follow the yellow public footpath arrows. The woodland track takes you along the top of the hill and back into woodland. Keep following the white arrows on trees and yellow public footpath signs. Continue on as the path curves, ignoring any paths off as the track turns into a gravel pathway and passes through Great Widmoor Wood. Keep an eye out for an Ordnance Survey Triangulation Pillar on your left as you follow the path.

❺ Cross the bridleway under a big oak tree and into Lordling Wood. The path continues to a metal farm gate and emerges onto a public byway with houses just off to the left.

❻ Turn right and follow the red public byway arrow downhill. The path then climbs before it levels out and emerges with fields on both sides, heading towards cottages and meeting a driveway. The driveway turns into the Chiltern Way on Furze Field Lane.

The Chilterns

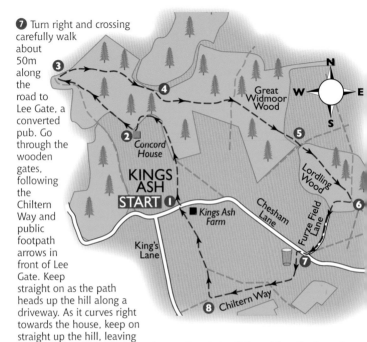

7 Turn right and crossing carefully walk about 50m along the road to Lee Gate, a converted pub. Go through the wooden gates, following the Chiltern Way and public footpath arrows in front of Lee Gate. Keep straight on as the path heads up the hill along a driveway. As it curves right towards the house, keep on straight up the hill, leaving the drive. You'll reach a metal gate, signed the Chiltern Way. Go through the gate into a large field. The path heads straight across for ¼ mile to a gap in the hedgeline.

8 Turn right and continue on the Chiltern Link footpath, with the hedge on your right. At the end of the field, the path leads you through a metal gate into a paddock. Follow the path diagonally across the paddock to a wooden gate first, then under powerlines to a metal kissing gate. Head through the gate, cross the farm track and go through the gate on the other side, closely following the yellow public footpath arrow and turning immediately left onto the concrete driveway which curves sharply to the right, out to the road where you'll find your car.

13 Great Missenden

2¼ miles (3.6 km)

Start: Park outside Missenden Abbey on London Road. There is plenty of roadside parking. **Postcode:** HP16 0BD.

OS Map: 181 Chiltern Hills North. **Grid Ref:** SP896010. **what3words:** rots.embarks.rave

Terrain: Begins with a long gentle incline up a quiet lane, before turning into woodland footpaths and grassy field tracks.

Refreshments: Head along Great Missenden High Street for The Cross Keys, where you'll find traditional pub dishes made from fresh local produce. ☎ 01494 865373. Alternatively, Matilda's Café Bistro serves wraps, burgers, milkshakes and more. ☎ 01494 890411.

HIGHLIGHTS

This is lovely wander through woodland and out over open fields, and across a railway line at the end. The route takes you past Gipsy House, where author Roald Dahl once lived, and wrote his famous stories. He wrote in a special hut in his garden, and there is a museum in his honour in the village which is well worth a visit if you have time.

THE WALK

1 From your parking spot, head to the gates of Missenden Abbey. Cross London Road to head up Whitefield Lane, which changes from a residential

The Chilterns

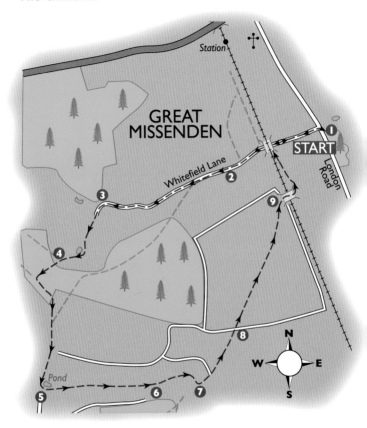

road into a country lane. Pass under the railway bridge and follow the lane as it winds up the hill.

2 As you reach the 10 mph sign, you'll see Gipsy House on your right, the former home of author Roald Dahl.

3 Follow the lane all the way to the top where it curves to the left. Follow the red public byway sign.

4 The track soon turns into a woodland path, past a rare breeds farm – keep an eye out for some sheep grazing in the fields. The path winds through the woods, through a conservation area and downhill, curving to the left across a really muddy patch and then ascends through the trees. Stick to the path as it emerges onto a tarmac driveway.

5 Turn left, and then on your left you'll see a lay-by and a pond which is worth exploring. Head down the tree-lined, paved driveway.

6 When you reach a fork in the driveway, take the left fork, curving round the edge of the property, keeping a laurel hedge on your right.

7 When you spot a wooden post and rail fence, turn left, past a green utility building on your right and the wooden fence on your left. The path goes downhill between paddocks and out to open grassland.

8 At the bottom of the hill, head straight across and up the other side, towards a lone hawthorn tree. In summer months you may well spot wild flowers, butterflies and other interesting insects through the meadow. Follow this path across the meadow and downhill again towards powerlines and a wooden gate.

9 Go through the gate, which leads you across a railway bridge, and continue on the path, ignoring the metal kissing gate on your right. The path runs parallel with the railway line, so keep an eye out for trains. The path emerges on Whitefield Lane. Turn right and head towards London Road and then to your car.

14 Little Kingshill
1¾ miles (3 km)

Start: Hare Lane, outside The Full Moon pub. **Postcode:** HP16 0EE.
OS Map: 172 Chiltern Hills East. **Grid Ref:** SU892990. **what3words:**
steady.blushed.swatting
Terrain: Woodland tracks, farm paths and a little walking on quiet
roads. Very muddy in wet weather.
Refreshments: At the start, The Full Moon pub and restaurant serves
classic pub food ☎ 01494 862397. Alternatively try the Barn Kitchen
at Peterley Manor Farm, on the route, where you'll find some of the
best Chilterns produce including their own homegrown harvest. On
offer is locally sourced food, including pizza, homemade cakes and
delicious afternoon teas. There is also indoor and outdoor seating
around a cosy fire pit. ☎ 01494 863566.

HIGHLIGHTS

This walk takes in farmland, a little woodland and Peterley Manor Farm,
which offers Pick Your Own fruit during summer months and grows Christmas
trees for the winter, as well as a fabulous farm shop, full of local produce.
It also has an award-winning café, the Barn Kitchen, which is well worth a

stop to sample some delicious local fare. You'll spot plenty of alpacas on the second half of the walk.

THE WALK

1 Walk across the front of the pub, between the seating area and pub doors, following the public footpath. The path narrows between a hedge and fence, leading to a metal kissing gate. Go through the gate and follow the path between two fields. After 500m, at the corner of Sandwich Wood, the path splits into two.

2 Take the left-hand fork, following the Chiltern Society Heritage Trail arrow. The path leads to a metal kissing gate at the corner of an arable field. Follow the path straight as it leads you across the field and towards farm buildings and the road beyond, under powerlines.

3 Exit the field through a metal gate, onto the driveway of Nairdwood Farm and turn right, away from the farm and onto the road. Immediately turn left and walk 350m carefully up the quiet Peterley Lane until you spot Peterley Manor Farm on your left.

4 Turn into the farm and continue straight. The path passes the farm shop, Barn Kitchen (definitely worth a visit) and fields. You may well spot your first alpacas here.

The Chilterns

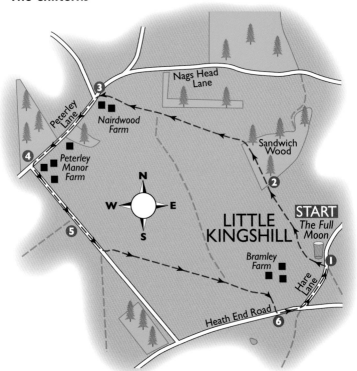

5 Head down the lane, following the blue public bridleway sign, for 100m and take the path on the left which soon opens out into alpaca fields. Follow the public footpath between fences. Once at the edge of the fields, the path heads right towards houses and emerges on their gravel driveways, through a metal gate. Follow the path to Heath End Road and turn left.

6 Walk down Heath End Road to Hare Lane. Turn left and follow the footpath back to your car.

15 Coleshill

2 miles (3 km)

Start: Barracks Hill, outside the church and Church Cottages where you'll find roadside parking. **Postcode:** HP7 0LN.
OS Map: 172 Chiltern Hills East. **Grid Ref:** SU947951. **what3words:** ducks.lies.elbow
Terrain: Woodland paths, some rutted with roots, gentle descents and one long incline up a track.
Refreshments: The Red Lion has a seasonal menu with local produce. Walker and dog friendly. ☎ 01494 723718.

HIGHLIGHTS

Starting in the pretty village of Coleshill, the walk takes in the surrounding fields before diving down to Winchmore Hill and the site of an historic chair-making business at Whielden Gate. The area is famous for furniture making, and three generations ran the workshop for nearly 100 years. You'll get some lovely Chiltern views as you climb, and a refreshment stop at the end.

THE WALK

❶ With your back to the church, walk along the Chiltern Way (signed), heading down the driveway to Lands Farm. The gravel drive leads you through a wooden gate and then a metal gate onto a concrete track. As it ends, continue on through a metal gate, taking you into a field.

47

The Chilterns

2 Leave the Chiltern Way at the fork, taking the right-hand path, through a gate and into a field. Head downhill, sticking to the right-hand side of the field, parallel to the wooden fence, following the public footpath. The path leads into the woods, before bringing you out beside another field. Continue on the public footpath as it leaves the field edge and takes you back into the woods on a narrow pathway. The path takes you deeper into the woods. Continue to follow the public footpath heading downhill through holly bushes.

3 The path leaves the woods through a wooden gate and heads downhill between two fields. Go through another gate which brings you out to a garage area. Head towards the road and just before you reach it, take the footpath on the left and follow that until it brings you out at Whielden Gate Farm, the site of a chair-making business for nearly 100 years until it burned down in the 1950s.

4 Continue along the road, walking on the grass verge for 65m until you reach a public footpath sign. Go through the metal gate and head diagonally right across the rough, flat area to the footpath in the corner which leads you uphill.

5 The track curves to the left, and when you reach the top of the hill, continue on, following the public footpath sign. The track hairpins to the right and continues up, before undulating between two fences.

6 At the end of the path, the track meets the Chiltern Way. Turn left and follow it for 50m, before leaving the Chiltern Way at the next marker post by turning right into the woods. There are white marker arrows on the trees, guiding you up the hill. The path leads you into a large arable field where you continue straight up and across it and down to a fenceline. Follow the edge of the field towards houses, then between hedges, emerging at Stock Grove on Barracks Hill.

7 Cross the road to the left, entering Coleshill Common, directly next to the Give Way sign. The path takes you through the woods, leading you uphill until you meet a path. Turn right and stick to this path as it heads out of the woods to a grassed area. Walk diagonally right across this grassy area towards a wooden bench, with the windmill beyond. When you reach the treeline and large oak tree with a picnic bench underneath, turn left and walk along the edge of the

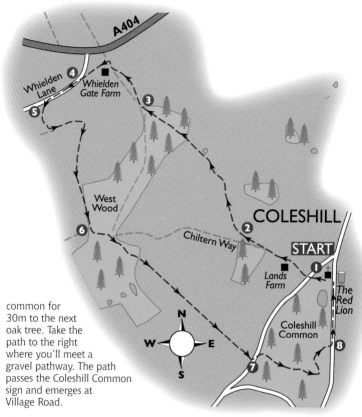

common for 30m to the next oak tree. Take the path to the right where you'll meet a gravel pathway. The path passes the Coleshill Common sign and emerges at Village Road.

8 Turn left and walk along the road, passing the pond on your left and The Red Lion on your right where you can stop for refreshments. After about 200m, take the path on your left, at the green garage marked Stony Path Cottage, just before the church, and emerge on Barracks Hill, where you'll find your car.

16 Hodgemoor Woods
2 miles (3.4 km)

Start: Hodgemoor Woods car park, Bottrells Lane. **Postcode:** HP8 4EQ.
OS Map: 172 Chiltern Hills East. **Grid Ref:** SU968938. **what3words:**
   fleet.broad.repair
Terrain: Woodland paths, muddy in wet weather.
Refreshments: None on the walk. The Harte and Magpies is a five-
   minute drive from the walk, on Amersham Road, where you'll find
   a good choice of light lunches and hearty meals. Dogs and wellies
   welcome. ☎ 01494 726754.

HIGHLIGHTS
Skirting the edge of the woodland, you'll see plenty of bluebells in the
spring and interesting remnants of buildings – less than 60 years ago the
woods were a resettlement camp, home to hundreds of Polish servicemen
and their families. You'll find concrete slabs and brickwork buried in the
woods, as well as an old pumping station to explore.

THE WALK
❶ With your back to the road, take the furthest footpath to your left. Go
through the wooden fences and follow the path as it runs parallel with the
road on your left. After 500m, the path passes through another wooden

fence, crosses a path and heads down a bridleway, marked by a white post and a horseshoe.

❷ 150m later, the path turns sharply to the right. Keep following the path past another bridleway sign marked 'Amber's Trail'. You'll start to descend, passing a sign for 'Spring Link' and the path curves to the left, becoming a small bridge. Follow it round to the left as it opens up out of the woods, with fields in front of you.

❸ At the edge of the woodland, turn right and follow the blue public bridleway sign as the path hugs the woods to your right.

❹ After 250m, at the corner of the final field, there's a turning back into the woods on your right. Take this and enter the woods again. You'll soon meet a T-junction. Take the left path, past a fallen tree with impressive roots. The path winds along the edge of the woods, past big craters and dips which are fun to explore. Some even have rope swings and abandoned evidence of the Polish resettlement camp that once stood here. After another 400m, you'll see a farm ahead of you on the other side of the fence.

❺ Follow the path as it curves round to the right, staying in the woods. In 100m it joins another path, slightly to the left, and after another 10m or so, take the left fork at the T-junction, continuing to follow the path round the edge of the woodland with the farmland on your left.

❻ After 100m the path joins the bridleway. Follow it round to the right, away from the road, under a telephone line and into the woods. As the path splits, continue along the bridleway on the left, following the yellow public footpath sign. Immediately on your left you'll see through the woods a disused pump house which is quite fun to explore, with old machinery inside.

❼ Continue up the path, passing bridleway signs and one marked 'Rawlings Dell' on your left, before you head downhill. As you reach the bottom of the hill, there are more fallen trees and dips to explore on your left. The bridleway crosses the valley, past the bridleway sign on your right.

❽ Turn right at the next footpath sign where there is a sign marked 'No Bridleway' with a crossed out horseshoe. 70m after that sign, you may be able to spot the remains of an old motorbike frame on your left, another

The Chilterns

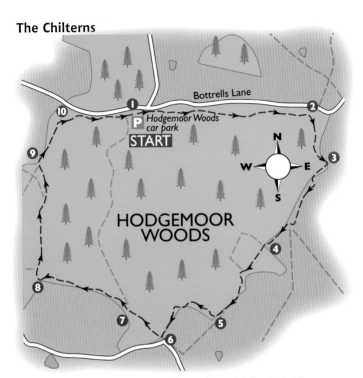

reminder of the wood's former residents. The path joins the bridleway once again. Continue straight on past a steep escarpment which you can pause at to explore.

9 150m on, the path converges with another and curves round to the right with a fence in front of you and the remains of a building behind it. Pass a small pond on the left and head uphill.

10 Just past the next bridleway sign you'll see a path on your right marked with a yellow and black arrow that takes you through ferns and foliage to the car park. This is a lovely spot for a picnic, with benches and green spaces to relax in.

17 Cholesbury

2¾ miles (4.3 km)

Start: Cholesbury Lane. Park in the lay-by outside Cholesbury Village Hall. **Postcode:** HP23 6ND.

OS Map: 181 Chiltern Hills North. **Grid Ref:** SP930070. **what3words:** interrupt.skater.lock

Terrain: Largely flat woodland paths and some farm track with one steep grassy ascent and descent towards the end.

Refreshments: The Full Moon serves freshly sourced food and ale on tap. Dog friendly. ☎ 01494 758959.

HIGHLIGHTS

One of the smallest villages in Buckinghamshire, Cholesbury's name refers to an Iron Age hillfort, built on the site of a Bronze Age settlement, which you'll walk through. There's also pretty woodland and farm tracks with some lovely views, including of Cholesbury Windmill, now a private residence.

THE WALK

❶ From the lay-by outside Cholesbury Village Hall, take the marked footpath to the left of it, through a wooden kissing gate and along the track. Pass through another kissing gate and along the left-hand edge of the field. You'll spot the church over a hedge to your left. Continue through the next

The Chilterns

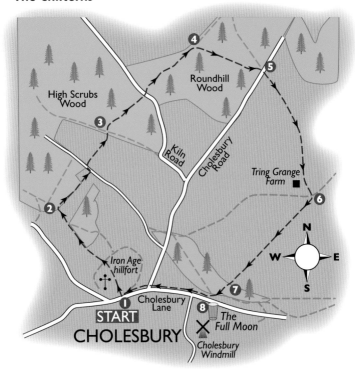

gate and across the next field, towards a metal farm gate. This area is part of the Iron Age hillfort, Cholesbury Camp, and as you go through the gate on the other side of the field, you'll cross the ditch that surrounds it. Once you've crossed the ditch, head straight on, following the public footpath which takes you into the woods. The path winds through the woods for about 200m, with a barbed wire fence to your left. At the fork, take the left path, sticking close to the fenceline. After 65m you'll reach a metal kissing gate. Go through the gate, through the next field, through another gate following the public footpath arrow and through another field. 100m on, a final metal kissing gate brings you into the woods.

2 Turn right here, following the footpath, with the field on your right. The path narrows before emerging onto a road. Turn left and walk about 25m along the road to a wooden kissing gate on the opposite side of the road. Go through the gate and head straight down the right side of the field, through the gate and into High Scrubs wood.

3 Cross another path, and follow the path ahead marked 'Footpath 12' into the woods. The path meanders through the woodland, before splitting. Take the right fork down to the road, cross carefully and go into Roundhill Wood. Stick to the main footpath, ignoring any splits or forks.

4 When you reach a yellow-tipped marker post, turn right on a wide woodland path with a bank on your right. The path leads you down to the road through the wooden chicane fence.

5 Cross the road, following the public bridleway sign onto a farm track marked Highcroft House and Tring Grange Farm. You may well spot some horses in the fields, and enjoy the beautiful rolling hills either side of the track. After just over 500m, the track passes Tring Grange Farm.

6 Pass the sign for Highcroft House and take the gate into a field on the right, marked public footpath, with a green arrow. Follow the path steeply up and over the field, keeping the hedge on your right. At the end of this field, pass through the metal kissing gate in front of you which leads you down a wide grassy track along the next field. As you walk, lift your gaze to spot Cholesbury Windmill in the distance. The grassy path starts to slope steeply downhill.

7 Towards the end of the slope, pass through a kissing gate and enter Cholesbury Common, continuing to the bottom of the hill. Cross the main path, following a public footpath arrow across and up the hill, into woodland. The path emerges from the woods opposite the windmill and Full Moon pub.

8 Turn right and over the common. As you pass, have a look at the memorial obelisks – one in celebration of Queen Victoria's Diamond Jubilee in 1897, and three puddingstones that mark the Diamond Jubilee of Queen Elizabeth II in 2012. Walking parallel to Cholesbury Lane, pass Hawridge and Cholesbury Cricket Club, cross the road and head back to your car.

18 Ley Hill

3 miles (4.8 km)

Start: Car park at Ley Hill Common next to the Beacon. **Postcode:** HP5 3QR.
OS Map: 181 Chiltern Hills North. **Grid Ref:** SP990019. **what3words:** pink.sing.table
Terrain: Flat but narrow footpaths, field and farm tracks. A few stiles.
Refreshments: The Crown serves traditional pub food. Dog and walker friendly. ☎ 01494 783910.

HIGHLIGHTS

With a history of brick making and pottery, you'll get a glimpse of the old orange clay pits as you skirt fields and tramp through woods, ending with some lovely views over the undulating Chiltern Hills.

THE WALK

❶ From the car park, head to the road in front of the pubs and turn left, keeping the pubs and houses on your right, and follow the quiet road to

Rowan Tree Farm, about 250m down the road. A public footpath arrow on the opposite side of the road indicates the path up Rowan Tree Farm's driveway. The drive turns into an unmade road and as it curves to the right, keep straight ahead, following the green public footpath sign.

2 The path leads you through the farmland between fences, keep an eye out for farm animals in their enclosures. At the end of the farm buildings, at the junction of multiple paths, cross the main track and keep straight into the woods beyond.

3 Before the sign for 'Cowcroft Wood', turn left and follow the public bridleway arrow. The path follows the edge of the fields on your left with the woods on your right. Continue on the bridleway, ignoring any paths that may lead off it. You'll pass a concrete Ordnance Survey trig point on your right as well as a huge badger sett. The path emerges at the corner of an arable field. Head straight to the bridleway and fenced footpath ahead. Continue straight on between the fences. On your left through the trees and in the distance, you'll see the orange clay of the old clay pit and brickworks.

4 The path curves sharply to the left corner of the field. Cross a wooden plank bridge and follow the path as it winds through the woods, keeping close to the arable field on your right. You'll reach a small stile – pass this and continue on the path. Reaching metal farm gates and a wooden five-bar gate on your right, pass through the wooden gate and cross to the footpath with the hedge on your right. At the edge of this field, go through the gate, cross the road and the stile opposite, into a field. Head down the right side of this grassy field, you'll see the estate of White End Park Farm on your right. Cross the stile in the corner of the field, cross the road, then over a stile into the next field.

5 Take the path in a straight line across the field, over a stile and into Codmore Wood, following the public footpath sign. The path winds through the woods to a track. Turn left and follow it to the footpath marker on the left. Take the public footpath across a wooden plank bridge. Cross the road and follow the public footpath on the opposite side of the road into the field, with the hedge on your left, downhill under power lines. In the corner of the field, immediately under the power lines the path heads downhill, following The Chiltern Society footpath sign to a stile on your left. Cross the stile into a field.

The Chilterns

6 Keep to the right side of the field, close to the hedge and fence line. The path takes you up and over the field and down the other side to a stile. Emerge onto Old School Hill next to Marylyn Cottage and turn right, following the road uphill.

7 Pass a lay-by on your left, Old School Cottage on your right, and as you reach Ashridge Farmhouse, there is a grassy pathway on your left that takes you across the golf course towards a clump of trees and a public footpath sign. Pass this sign and keep to the edge of the golf course, you should be able to see your car and the pub appear from behind the trees.

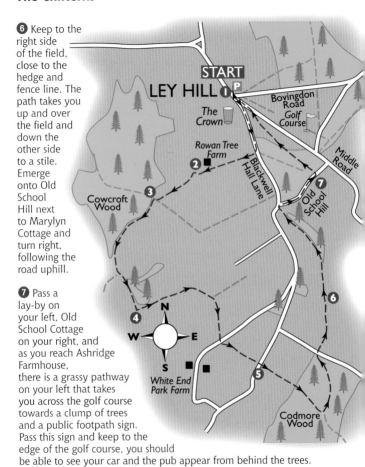

19 **Dunstable Downs**

3½ miles (5.4 km)

> **Start:** Chilterns Gateway Centre car park (NT), or walkers' car park
> further along the B4541. **Postcode:** LU6 2GY.
> **OS Map:** 181 Chiltern Hills North. **Grid Ref:** TL008197. **what3words:**
> vast.rats.ranged (main car park) acid.food.boss (walkers' car park).
> **Terrain:** Field paths with one very steep descent and ascent.
> **Refreshments:** The Chilterns Gateway Centre is walker and dog friendly,
> serving a wide range of hot and cold drinks, hot food, sandwiches and
> delicious cakes. ☎ 01582 500920.

HIGHLIGHTS

Providing stunning views across the Downs and surrounding area, this walk
also takes in Whipsnade Tree Cathedral, a collection of trees and shrubs
planted in the form of a medieval cathedral.

THE WALK

❶ From the walkers' car park, take the path to the left, past the information
board. This is the Icknield Way Trail. Reach the large metal sculpture, and
turn left. If you're starting at the Chilterns Gateway Centre, walk down the
left side of the building to the metal sculpture and turn left.

The Chilterns

2 Leave the paved path, onto the grass and to the right side of the hedge, slightly downhill, following signs for the Chiltern Way, keeping the hedge on your left. Go through the metal gate, keeping close to the fence.

3 Pass through the next metal gate on your left, following the blue Chiltern Way bridleway sign, then continue straight ahead across a tarmac drive, following a green sign indicating The Icknield Way public bridleway. Continue following the public bridleway sign into the woods. The path leads you out past Evergreen Lodge. Continue down the driveway and past Sallowsprings.

4 As the fence ends, turn left, entering Sallowsprings nature reserve. Follow the path to the corner of the field and into a wooded area, curving round to the right. Take the right-hand fork as you stick to the edge of the field, keeping the fence on your left. The path emerges onto the tarmac drive. Continue for another 100m to the National Trust marker for Whipsnade.

5 Turn right, following the Chiltern Way bridleway blue arrow. You'll reach Whipsnade Tree Cathedral. Turn left before this, skirting round the outside of it to the QE2 Jubilee Orchard. You'll see a carved column indicating the orchard on your left.

6 Go straight on through the wooden fenceline and turn immediately right, walking through Whipsnade Tree Cathedral car park to the wooden gate on the opposite side. Enter the Tree Cathedral and follow Icknield Way yellow arrows around the edge to a gap in the fence and a metal kissing gate, leading you across a field. A metal kissing gate takes you down to a footpath.

7 Turn right following the Icknield Way, past Observatory Lodge, for 700m. The path brings you out at a viewpoint.

8 The path curves to a yellow-topped marker post on your right. Head to the left of it and take the main path downhill. A 'Steep Slope' sign on your right warns you of what's to come! You'll meet a wooden fence on your left, and then steps lead you down the steep hill. At the end of the steps, the path continues steeply downhill, passing gates on your right, and a glimpse of the road on your left.

9 The path curves to the right between hedgerows, away from the road and gently undulates around the foot of the hill for about ½ mile. Ignore any paths off, keeping the hedge on your left.

10 The path starts to ascend again, passing through a wooden fenceline and curves round to the right, with a National Trust oak leaf post on your left and a gate on your right. The path leads away and up the hill. You'll soon see a metal kissing gate on your right with a red arrow on a post. Follow the red arrow up the hill. As the path emerges in a wide open space, you'll spot the walkers' car park at the top of the hill. If you're parked there, head to your car, or turn right and follow the paved footpath to the big metal sculpture, and left to the Chilterns Gateway Centre.

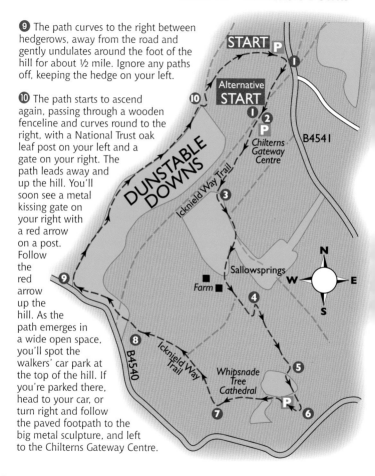

20 Little Gaddesden

1¾ miles (3 km)

Start: The Church of St Peter and St Paul. Free parking along the road.
   Postcode: HP4 1NZ.
OS Map: 181 Chiltern Hills North. **Grid Ref:** SP997137. **what3words:**
   flattery.abolish.angel
Terrain: Flat across fields and footpaths. Plenty of gates.
Refreshments: The Bridgewater Arms serves classic pub food and roasts
   on a Sunday. Family and dog friendly. ☎ 01442 842408.

HIGHLIGHTS

A gentle, flat wander around the village of Little Gaddesden. Plenty of
sheep, ponies and goats to spot in the fields, and a pub perfectly placed
halfway round. Little Gaddesden is situated on the Ashridge estate in the
Chilterns Area of Outstanding Natural Beauty and is managed by the
National Trust. The area has appeared in many TV programmes and films,
and has a number of famous faces who live here.

THE WALK

1 Walk up Church Road, past the church to the metal farm gate at the bend in the road. Go through the metal kissing gate and into the field, following the public footpath sign. Cross the field to the hedgeline on the other side. Pass through the gate on the opposite side of the field, following the public footpath sign and head down the left-hand edge of the next arable field.

2 At the end of the field, take a sharp right and almost double back on yourself, heading diagonally across the field under the large oak tree, on the Chiltern Way. Continue on the footpath to the end of the field.

3 Go through the metal kissing gate and into a grassy field. Continue following the Chiltern Way footpath signs. Cross the field, heading towards the wooden gate on the opposite side. Pass through the gate and cross the next field, heading for the wooden gate that will lead you out onto the road.

4 Carefully cross the quiet lane, following the green Chiltern Way arrow, directing you to a footpath and gate on the opposite side of the road, diagonally to your left. The gate leads you into a field, and the footpath winds across it. Go through the wooden kissing gate on the other side of the field and continue straight on the path with houses to your left. There's plenty of livestock to spot – goats, sheep, horses and ponies are dotted about the fields.

5 The path emerges onto a road. Turn right and head up the footpath, past the Bridgewater Arms. Stop here for a refreshment break if you wish. There are some beautiful old buildings here, so take your time as you walk along the road to have a look at the architecture. Pass the village shop, and 150m on, as the road starts to bend to the left, you'll see a public footpath signposted to Hudnall Corner.

6 Follow the path through the wooden gate on your right, then immediately turn right, through the big wooden farm gate, following the public footpath across the field, heading for the metal gate on the opposite side. Go through the gate, and head across the next field, through another metal gate into a pasture where there may well be sheep grazing. Walk across this field, under oak trees to the edge of the field. Pass through another gate into the final

The Chilterns

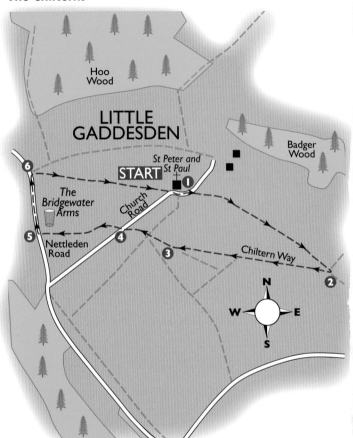

field, heading straight towards the church, looking for a wooden gate in the hedge. The path leads you by the church car park, to the road where you should find your car.